LIVING UNSHAKEABLE IN A SHAKING WORLD

6 Principles for successful kingdom living

Dr. John Polis

LIVING UNSHAKEABLE IN A SHAKING WORLD
6 Principles For Successful Kingdom Living
By John Polis

ISBN: 9798602776997

All Rights Reserved. No part of this publication may be produced or transmitted in any form or by any means without written permission of the author. The author guarantees all contents are original and do not infringe upon the legal rights of any other person or work.

Prepared for Publication By

PUBLISHING

MAKING YOUR BOOK A REALITY

Cedar Point, NC | 843-929-8768 | info@BandBpublishingLLC.com

Scripture quotations marked NKJV are taken from the New King James Version®. Copyright © 1982 by Thomas Nelson. Used by permission. All rights reserved.

Scripture quotations marked NIV are taken from THE HOLY BIBLE, NEW INTERNATIONAL VERSION®, NIV® Copyright © 1973, 1978, 1984, 2011 by Biblica, Inc.® Used by permission. All rights reserved worldwide.

Scripture quotations marked KJV are taken from The Holy Bible, King James Version.

Scripture quotations marked NLT are taken from the Holy Bible, New Living Translation, copyright © 1996, 2004, 2015 by Tyndale House Foundation. Used by permission of Tyndale House Publishers, Inc., Carol Stream, Illinois 60188. All rights reserved.

To Contact the Author
JOHN POLIS MINISTRIES
PO BOX 1007 | Beaufort, SC 29901
drjohn@rfiusa.org
www.rfiusa.org

CONTENTS

THE DISCIPLESHIP SERIES 1
What is it & how to use it.

INTRODUCTION 5
Living Unshakeable In A Shaking World

KINGDOM PRINCIPLE #1 11
Follow the Right People

KINGDOM PRINCIPLE #2 23
Feed Your Faith

KINGDOM PRINCIPLE #3 39
Find Your Purpose

KINGDOM PRINCIPLE #4 53
Forsake Sin

KINGDOM PRINCIPLE #5 65
Fit Into the Body of Christ

KINGDOM PRINCIPLE #6 75
Fix Your Heart

THE DISCIPLESHIP SERIES

WHAT IS IT & HOW TO USE IT.

The **BE STRONG IN THE LORD: Discipleship Series** contains handpicked books written by John Polis that are designed to help you grow in spiritual maturity as you follow Jesus Christ and learn to apply the Word of God to your life. In this resource, you will receive revelation knowledge of key principles enabling you to survive and thrive during the worst storms of life. This resource is great for personal devotion time and/or small group studies.

If you desire to use this for small group study, it will work best if everyone in the group has their own book to answer and grow through together. More copies can be resourced at JohnPolis.com

HOW TO USE THIS RESOURCE

This discipleship resource, **LIVING UNSHAKEABLE IN A SHAKING WORLD,** is designed to be used over a **SIX-WEEK** period. Each week has several elements that will help you get the most out of the subject being discussed. Here are the elements and a brief description of each.

 **READ:** Day one of every chapter has a reading portion. This introduces and provides scriptural support for the topic.

 **INSIGHT:** Also on day one, an INSIGHT question is presented for reflection and application.

 **WATCH:** Day two of each chapter there is a video from the author, Dr. John Polis. He briefly shares more on the topic of the chapter. Videos can be viewed by going to johnpolis.com, clicking on **DISCIPLESHIP SERIES** on the main menu.

 **MEMORIZE:** Day three of each chapter, you will learn the related scripture through writing, MEMORIZATION, and sharing it with a friend. The Word of God must be one of the highest priorities for a follower of Jesus!

 **ACTION STEP:** Day four of each chapter, there will be a question that will help you put action to what you have been learning.

 **TRANSFER:** Day five of each chapter, you will write a brief summary of what God has shown you throughout the week, and then you will choose one person to share it with.

 **REFLECTION:** Day six of each chapter, review your previous responses and REFLECT over what God has shown you throughout the topic study. Include any results of your ACTION STEP. As leadership expert John Maxwell says, *"Experience is not the best teacher, evaluated experience is".*

INTRODUCTION

LIVING UNSHAKEABLE IN A SHAKING WORLD

Various places in the Bible God says that there will be great shaking in the earth and among the nations, and we're living in such time right now.

"See that you do not refuse Him who speaks. For if they did not escape who refused Him who spoke on earth, much more shall we not escape if we turn away from Him who speaks from heaven, whose voice then shook the earth; but now He has promised, saying, "Yet once more I shake not only the earth, but also heaven." Now this, "Yet once more," indicates the removal of those things that are being shaken, as of things that are made, that the

things which cannot be shaken may remain. Therefore, since we are receiving a kingdom which cannot be shaken, let us have grace, by which we may serve God acceptably with reverence and godly fear. For our God is a consuming fire." Hebrews 12:25-29 NKJV

God says that a part of the shaking that will take place in the world and in our lives is to help the emerging kingdom of God come forth in the earth. Everything that's not derived from or attached to the kingdom of God will eventually perish, it will fall away, but the Bible says *"we have received a kingdom which cannot be shaken."*

I want to offer six kingdom principles that will attach us to the eternal, unshakable kingdom of God and thereby make our life unshakeable as well. I believe we can still be standing when there is a whole lot of shaking going on, and we can be, and we will be if we tap into these six principles that this book is about.

In Second Thessalonians chapter 2, Paul says,

"Now, brethren, concerning the coming of our Lord Jesus Christ and our gathering together to Him, we ask you, not to be soon shaken in mind or troubled, either by spirit or by word

or by letter, as if from us, as though the day of Christ had come. Let no one deceive you by any means; for that Day will not come unless the falling away comes first, and the man of sin is revealed, the son of perdition," 2 Thessalonians 2:1-3 NKJV

What had shaken these people was that someone had told them that Jesus had already returned to the earth, and they had missed it, and their loved ones had missed it. Paul said that wasn't true, that there were many things that had to happen before the Lord returns, so don't let these things shake you.

Paul is saying we need to take a posture of not being shaken in mind, or in our hearts, either by any spirit that may attack us or try to influence, or any word that may be spoken, or any source whatsoever. We're to live an unshakeable life, and that means after everything is shaken away that doesn't find its source and its roots in God, those that are attached to God and established in His principles will still be there.

My wife Rebecca and I have been serving Jesus now for 36 years and we've seen a whole lot of shaking going on in a lot of places and a lot of different ways, and I can assure you that following the principles I'm giving you have enabled us to remain unshaken no matter what goes on. That's the potential we all have as Christians, to live an unshakable life.

These principles will also make you a person of influence to others around you. When their life is going to pieces and they don't know what to do, they will see your stability and steadfastness, and the quality and character of your life. They look at you and they say, "*what are you doing to keep your peace and joy?*" And then you can tell them, "*I've been born again, and I'm living and seeking first the kingdom of God and His righteousness and all things are being added to me; what have I got to worry about? I'm attached to the eternal, unshakeable principles of the kingdom. After everything is said and done, there is only one thing that's going to remain and that is the kingdom of God. Heaven and earth will pass away but His Word will never pass away.*"

The six kingdom principles that I want to give you will help you to be steadfast and not be moved in the time of difficulty; and believe me, the years ahead are going to have many opportunities for you to get troubled and shaken. But God is working out His plan; He has it all in His hand. He is not in heaven wringing His hands, calling the angels together and saying, "*hey, what are we going to do?*" He has had a plan from the foundation of the world, and He's going to bring that plan to pass and He's going to use you and me to do it, so be encouraged today.

You might be going through shaking right now in your marriage, your job, your finances, and maybe your health, and Jesus told us to expect these things in a world where troubles come. But He also said, *"be of good cheer for I have overcome the world."* (John 16:33).

There is something eternal for you to base your life upon and attach your heart and mind to, the principles of God's Word, the teachings of the kingdom. When you are born again, you can begin living by kingdom principles. That means you and I can have a life that resembles Jesus' life. And would you agree with me, He wasn't shook up; He wasn't falling apart; He wasn't on anti-depressants. Jesus didn't depend upon anything except the very kingdom principles He came to teach us. So let's begin our journey to living unshakable in a shaking world.

DR. JOHN POLIS

KINGDOM PRINCIPLE #1

FOLLOW THE RIGHT PEOPLE

Hebrews 13:7 NLT
"Remember your leaders who taught you the Word of God. Think of all the good that has come from their lives, and follow the example of their faith."

DR. JOHN POLIS

DAY 1

If we're going to live an unshakable life, we have to follow the right people in our life. The Bible says,

> *"Remember your leaders who taught you the Word of God. Think of all the good that has come from their lives, and follow the example of their faith." Hebrews 13:7 NLT*

A Christian leader should always set the example for others to follow.

Conversely, in a major news network report, one of the top sports figures, the kind of person that everybody thought was the ideal home grown boy, was married and, at the same time, maintained relationships with multiple mistresses. The news media were talking about how this person's conduct will affect all the people who looked to him as a role model. The reporter went on to suggest that people should focus on the person's athletic skills and not his personal life, referring to his character. This is why it is important for parents to help their children find the right kind of role models.

THINK OF THE FUTURE

We have to think about what the world will look like that our children and grandchildren will be living in. We need to be teaching the kingdom principle of following the right people. Don't make heroes and idols out of anybody, including popular TV preachers, politicians, and sports figures. We can learn from the skills, abilities, and talents of such people, but when it comes to the example of character, the Bible tells us clearly that we are to look to spiritual leaders.

There is a very wise saying: "*your gifts can take you very high but only your character will keep you there.*" The Bible says,

> "Therefore let him who thinks he stands take heed lest he fall." 1 Corinthians 10:12 NKJV

PAUL LIVED AN UNSHAKEABLE LIFE

In Philippians 4:9, the Apostle Paul said to his followers in Philippi,

"The things which you learned and received and heard and saw in me, these do, and the God of peace will be with you." Philippians 4:9 NKJV

In essence Paul was saying, *"If you'll listen to me and do what I do and follow my wisdom and instruction, and learn the principles that I have learned about the kingdom of God, the God of peace will be with you as well!"*

Paul had the God of peace with him, didn't he? The God of Shalom. The Hebrew word *shalom* means complete in well-being, soundness, wholeness. When the Hebrews would say "*shalom*," they were saying "*be made whole, be complete in number, be at rest.*" The Apostle Paul went through a whole lot of shaking in his life, including jail time, being beaten, shipwrecked, and left for dead. But at the end of the day he said, "*The God of peace has been with me.*" Paul left this world having finished his course, living an unshakeable life all of us can follow.

The God of peace wants to manifest Himself to you, with you, and in you. But there are some things you've got to do; you've got to learn to live the principles of the kingdom of God from others who have followed Christ before you.

ELDERS IN THE CHURCH & PARENTS

God's Word tells us that the elders of the church were to be examples to the flock of God (1 Peter 5:3). It's vitally important that we have an active relationship with our local church leaders who are godly and are spiritually mature role models in our life. Like the Bible says, *"know them that labor among you"* (1 Thessalonians 5:12). We need firsthand knowledge, seeing our leader when the chips are down and how they respond, how they walk in faith through their circumstances.

This type of example should be happening in our own homes as well. Parents should be the number one spiritual leaders in the household and elders should be the number one spiritual leaders in the church.

THE MATURING PROCESS

"This is a faithful saying: If a man desires the position of a bishop, he desires a good work." (This refers to an elder as well.) *"A bishop then must be blameless, the husband of one wife, temperate, sober-minded, of good behavior, hospitable, able to teach; not given to wine, not violent, not greedy for money, but gentle, not quarrelsome, not covetous; one who*

rules his own house well, having his children in submission with all reverence (for if a man does not know how to rule his own house, how will he take care of the church of God?); not a novice, lest being puffed up with pride he fall into the same condemnation as the devil. Moreover he must have a good testimony among those who are outside, lest he fall into reproach and the snare of the devil." 1 Timothy 3:1-7 NKJV

It is not a wise practice to put people that are new to the faith into high levels of spiritual leadership because they have not had enough time to go through any maturing process. In their immaturity, they could then be tempted to be puffed up with pride. When you have a process that you go through to become a spiritual leader, then you're there because you qualified. On the other hand, when you give away titles and positions to people, then they may feel that there is something special about them since they didn't have to go through the process, and this can result in a prideful spirit. *True spiritual leadership seeks out any process that promotes growth in spiritual character and maturity.* These leaders then become an example to God's people. That kind of leadership, that kind of example, is what we need more than anything else in today's world.

An exemplary life doesn't happen overnight. It takes some chiseling, some hammering; it takes going through the winepress. It involves a lot for our life to come to the place where it's an example to other people. But after a person goes through the maturing process, then they will have credibility and people will want to follow their example.

To begin living an unshakeable life, we must apply Principle #1, which is FOLLOW THE RIGHT PEOPLE.

IDENTIFY A MATURE SPIRITUAL LEADER THAT GOD HAS PUT INTO YOUR LIFE AND TWO QUALITIES IN THEM ARE WORTH FOLLOWING.

_____

_____

_____

_____

_____

DAY 2

Watch today's video by going to johnpolis.com, clicking on *Discipleship Series* in the main menu and then choosing **LIVING UNSHAKEABLE IN A SHAKING WORLD** Week 1.

WHAT STOOD OUT TO YOU AND WHAT IS GOD SHOWING YOU THROUGH THE VIDEO?

_____

_____

_____

_____

_____

_____

_____

DAY 3

Write **HEBREWS 13:7** in your favorite translation. Go over this passage several times until you can say it from memory and then share it with one person by the end of the day.

HEBREWS 13:7

_____

_____

_____

_____

_____

_____

WHO DID YOU QUOTE YOUR VERSE TO?

_____

DAY 4

WHAT IS ONE AREA OF YOUR LEADER'S LIFE THAT YOU WOULD LIKE TO BECOME MORE LIKE AND WHAT MUST CHANGE IN YOUR LIFE TO MAKE ROOM FOR THAT NEW QUALITY?

_____

_____

_____

_____

_____

_____

_____

_____

_____

_____

DAY 5

IN JUST A FEW SENTENCES, WRITE DOWN WHAT YOU HAVE LEARNED IN THIS CHAPTER AND THEN SHARE IT WITH ONE PERSON BY THE END OF THE DAY.

_____

_____

_____

_____

_____

_____

_____

WHO DID YOU SHARE WITH WHAT YOU LEARNED?

_____

DAY 6

Take time to review everything you have written down that God has shown to you throughout the week. You can also write down any results from your **ACTION STEP**. As leadership expert John Maxwell says, *"Experience is not the best teacher, evaluated experience is"*.

_____

_____

_____

_____

_____

_____

_____

_____

KINGDOM PRINCIPLE #2

FEED YOUR FAITH

2 Timothy 2:15 KJV
"Study to shew thyself approved unto God, a workman that needeth not to be ashamed, rightly dividing the word of truth."

DAY 1

The late Reverend Dr. Lester Sumrall, a great general in the church and in the kingdom, once said, *"feed your faith and you will starve your doubts to death."*

You have to intentionally feed your faith, and this takes some effort. You have to be a hearer and a doer of the Word.

> *"But why do you call Me 'Lord, Lord,' and not do the things which I say? Whoever comes to Me, and hears My sayings and does them, I will show you whom he is like: He is like a man building a house, who dug deep and laid the foundation on the rock. And when the flood arose, the stream beat vehemently against that house, and could not shake it, for it was founded on the rock. Luke 6:46-48 NKJV*

In this verse, when it comes to feeding our faith, we can see three things are necessary to develop a life that is unshakable.

1. "Whoever comes to Me"

2. "and hears My sayings"

3. "and does them".

You have to come to Jesus because if you don't come to Jesus, you're not building your life on the right foundation. When you come to Him, you get born again; you repent of your sins, and you make Jesus Christ the Lord of your life. That's the starting point for you to begin to build an unshakable life. Remember, Christ is the chief cornerstone, our sure foundation. When you get connected to Christ, you begin the building of your life upon eternal, unshakeable principles. This active relationship with Jesus is critical and the first step to living an unshakeable life.

A lot of people take the first step in coming to Jesus, and then they stop. Jesus didn't say to stop there, He said, *"and hears My sayings and does them"* We are called to be practicing Christians, not Christians in name only. A practicing Christian is both a hearer and a doer of the Word.

So Jesus says: *"you come, you hear, you do!"* Then He said,

> *"Whoever comes to Me, and hears My sayings and does them, I will show you whom he is like: He is like a man building a house, who*

dug deep and laid the foundation on the rock. And when the flood arose, [when the shaking started], *the stream beat vehemently against that house,* [against that life], *and could not shake it, for it was founded on the rock. But he who heard and did nothing* [in other words, in one ear and out the other and didn't apply the principles to their life] *is like a man who built a house on the earth without a foundation, against which the stream beat vehemently; and immediately it fell. And the ruin of that house was great." Luke 6:47-49 NKJV*

This person was, in presumption, not faith. He said *"well I know what the Bible says, I'm not doing it, but I know what the Bible says."* Just knowing what the Bible says will still get you destroyed when the floods come. It's being a doer of what the Bible said that makes you unshakeable and connects you to the eternal foundation, the eternal truth.

The passage says, *"the stream beat vehemently."* Some storms can be vehement, can't they? *"And immediately the house fell and the ruin of that house was great."* To prevent this, you have to feed your faith!

HOW DO YOU FEED YOUR FAITH?

The Bible says that the man dug deep and laid his foundation upon a rock. Digging deep means putting forth the effort. On the other hand, a shallow person is looking for the easy way, for what's laying on top of the ground. This person says, *"I'll take it, but I'm not going to put any extra effort into trying to find it."* If you're the type of person that has come to Jesus but you want everything to be easy and handed to you; *"if God speaks to me fine, if He doesn't okay too".* Then perhaps you didn't understand what coming to Jesus really means.

Coming to Jesus is not a take it or leave it deal. God said we are to go after Him and seek His face, and seek Him with passion and with all of our heart; come after Him and say, *"here I am Lord, speak to me".* **You can't be a casual Christian and have an unshakeable life,** you can't be a Christian that is just looking for convenience and an easy way. You have to realize that in order for your faith to become strong, to dissolve the doubts in your life, and cause you to be unshakeable in the midst of vehement storms, you have to go beyond the surface and get deep. That means you've got to be a student of the Word of God.

"Study to shew thyself approved unto God,

a workman that needeth not to be ashamed, rightly dividing the word of truth." 2 Timothy 2:15 KJV

BECOME A STUDENT

The disciples were pupils of Jesus hanging on His every word. They sat when He sat, when He stood up, they stood up, when He went walking, they went walking, wherever He was they were, because they wanted to hear everything coming out of His mouth. Jesus is not here bodily for you to go find Him and sit down with Him, but the Bible says in Ephesians 4, "*When He ascended on high... He gave gifts unto men.*" God has put ministry gifts in the church; the fivefold ministry gifts of apostle, prophet, evangelist, pastor, and teacher (Ephesians 4:11), and He speaks through these ministry gifts to His church. Find those gifts, those men and those women of God and sit with them, be where they are, hear what they've got to say, follow their faith, follow their example. That's why the local church is so important. God set the church up and put the ministry gifts in it so you'd have a place to come, to hear, and to do as Jesus said and did.

This is what we have to understand. We cannot take or leave church; because we're evading God's way of dealing with our life and speaking to us. It's not that He doesn't speak to us individually when we go before Him, He does; or when we get in the Word, He does. But that is not the only way He speaks. One of the primary ways He speaks to us is through the ministry gifts, otherwise let's shut the doors and all go home and read our Bibles. God established the local church and gave the ministry gifts to it for the specific purpose of feeding your faith.

BECOME A GIVER

The Bible says, *"It's more blessed to give than it is to receive,"* so you don't want to always be on the receiving end. You want to grow and get in on the giving end. That means to grow to the place where you can start sharing the Word of God. You don't need a church pulpit to do that. Kenneth Hagin used to preach to cabbage heads. He said that he would go out in the garden, stand on a box and preach to cabbage heads. He didn't care, he just wanted to preach the Word of God.

PREPARE YOURSELF TO HEAR

When you come to the house of God, you should not only pray for yourself, but you pray for the spiritual leader who will be ministering to you. Pray, *"God I'm coming to hear, put Your Word in the man or woman of God's mouth, I want to hear You through them.*" When you are faithful in following this preparation, you'll be sitting there and you will find yourself in the cloud of God's glory. God will speak something to you miles beyond what you have just heard. What an awesome experience when we recognize that God is speaking directly to us!

LOGOS & RHEMA

There are a couple of Greek words translated into one English word, "Word". When you read the Bible every place it says "the word of God," it may have different meanings, depending upon the context. The first is "LOGOS", it is just a word for the Bible in general, the whole Word of God. For example, John 1:1: "*in the beginning was the Word.*", John 1:14 "*Jesus was the Word made flesh*", "if you've seen Me you've seen the Father." The Word of God – logos, refers to the total concept of God.

The second is the Greek word "RHEMA" which means the spoken Word. It is when you are reading or listening to the "LOGOS" that God speaks directly to you. God speaking is the "RHEMA", going from information to revelation; and it's revelation, not just information that causes your faith to grow. Jesus said in Matthew 4:4,

> *"It is written, 'Man shall not live by bread alone, but by every word* [Rhema] *that proceeds from the mouth of God.'"* Matthew 4:4 NKJV

When you hear the voice of God through His Word, that's what gives you life, that's what pumps faith into your heart. This is what I have referred to earlier as digging deep. This is going the extra mile, putting in the extra effort not just looking for whatever is laying on the surface or pulling a promise for the day out of your promise box. You might get a little nugget laying on top of the ground like that; but when you get your good study Bible and your note pad, some good Bible software, and get plugged into the local church, you're on the way to spiritual maturity, to becoming a disciple able to reproduce yourself in others that they too may know Christ. When you undergird these things with a private devotion time, you will find yourself satisfied but increasingly hungry. The more of God you get, the more you want.

REVELATION MAKES US UNSHAKEABLE

In Matthew 16:13, we find Jesus asking His disciples a very important question:

"...'Who do men say that I, the Son of Man, am?' So they said, 'Some say John the Baptist, some Elijah, and others Jeremiah or one of the prophets.' He said to them, 'But who do you say that I am?' Simon Peter answered and said, 'You are the Christ, the Son of the living God.' " Matthew 16:13-16 NKJV

How did Peter get the right answer? How are you going to get the right answer? How are you going to answer the problems of life when they come your way? How are you going to answer the devil? How are you going to answer sickness, disease, poverty, and all the problems we face? How are we going to answer the circumstances of life?

"Jesus answered and said to him, 'Blessed are you, Simon Bar-Jonah, for flesh and blood has not revealed this to you, but My Father who is in heaven. And I also say to you that you are Peter, and on this rock [the rock of truth, the rock of revelation of who Christ is], *I will build My church, and the gates of Hades shall not prevail against it.' " Matthew 16:17-18 NKJV*

Peter didn't come to the knowledge of who Christ was by himself, but by the revelation given to him by God. Every revelation is another rock in your spiritual foundation.

The important thing is to get from simply information to revelation. This revelation knowledge is what makes you unshakeable in a shaking world.

NAME ONE RHEMA OR REVELATION THAT GOD SHARED WITH YOU FROM HIS WORD AND HOW IT MADE YOU MORE UNSHAKEABLE?

_____

_____

_____

_____

_____

_____

_____

_____

_____

_____

DAY 2

Watch today's video by going to johnpolis.com, clicking on *Discipleship Series* in the main menu and then choosing **LIVING UNSHAKEABLE IN A SHAKING WORLD** Week 2.

WHAT STOOD OUT TO YOU AND WHAT IS GOD SHOWING YOU THROUGH THE VIDEO?

_____

_____

_____

_____

_____

_____

_____

DAY 3

Write **2 TIMOTHY 2:15** in your favorite translation. Go over this passage several times until you can say it from memory and then share it with one person by the end of the day.

2 TIMOTHY 2:15

_____

_____

_____

_____

_____

_____

WHO DID YOU QUOTE YOUR VERSE TO?

_____

DAY 4

WHAT WAYS CAN YOU PRIORITIZE SPENDING TIME IN GOD'S WORD?

_____

_____

_____

_____

_____

_____

_____

_____

_____

_____

DAY 5

IN JUST A FEW SENTENCES, WRITE DOWN WHAT YOU HAVE LEARNED IN THIS CHAPTER AND THEN SHARE IT WITH ONE PERSON BY THE END OF THE DAY.

_____

_____

_____

_____

_____

_____

_____

WHO DID YOU SHARE WITH WHAT YOU LEARNED?

_____

DAY 6

Take time to review everything you have written down that God has shown to you throughout the week. You can also write down any results from your **ACTION STEP**. As leadership expert John Maxwell says, *"Experience is not the best teacher, evaluated experience is"*.

_____

_____

_____

_____

_____

_____

_____

_____

KINGDOM PRINCIPLE #3

FIND YOUR PURPOSE

John 4:33-34. NKJV
"Therefore the disciples said to one another, 'Has anyone brought Him anything to eat?' Jesus said to them, 'My food is to do the will of Him who sent Me, and to finish His work.'"

DAY 1

The third principle is to find your purpose. Jesus knew His purpose. He lived life on purpose. Life wasn't an accident for Him, a series of coincidences, He was on a mission.

In John 4, we have the story of Jesus in Samaria and the woman at the well. Jesus had sent His disciples into the nearby village to get some food. While they were gone, He struck up a conversation with the Samaritan woman who had come to the well for water. When the disciples returned, they urged Jesus,

> "Meanwhile his disciples urged him, 'Rabbi, eat something.' But he said to them, 'I have food to eat that you know nothing about.'"
> John 4:31-32 NIV

The disciples wondered what kind of food Jesus was talking about.

> *"Therefore the disciples said to one another, 'Has anyone brought Him anything to eat?' Jesus said to them, 'My food is to do the will of Him who sent Me, and to finish His work.'"*
> *John 4:33-34. NKJV*

PURPOSE BRINGS STRENGTH

The King James Version says *"My meat is to do the will of Him who sent Me."* Biblically speaking, meat or solid food is for them that are of a full age. Meat is what gives you strength. Jesus said *"My meat,* [what feeds Me and sustains Me, and makes Me strong] *is to do the will of God."* One of the characteristics of a mature person is that they have identified God's will and purpose for their life, and have then taken responsibility for it, and that's when the strength comes.

When you have purpose in your heart, there is a faith that rises within you: *"I'm unshakeable because I know I'm in the will of God; I'm in the plan and purpose of God for my life, and let it come, whatever the devil is going to throw against me, the God of peace is with me, I'm in my place, I'm in my purpose and I cannot be moved, no weapon formed against me will prosper! Why? I have confidence from knowing I'm in God's will for me, I'm operating in my God-designed purpose."* There is an unshakeableness that comes in your spirit when you know you are in your God-given purpose.

OUR PURPOSE

In John 4:34, Jesus shares His purpose, *"My meat is to do the will of Him that sent Me and to finish His work."* Then He shares with the disciples their purpose,

> *"Do you not say, 'There are still four months and then comes the harvest'? Behold, I say to you, lift up your eyes and look at the fields, for they are already white for harvest! And he who reaps receives wages, and gathers fruit for eternal life, that both he who sows and he who reaps may rejoice together. For in this the saying is true: 'One sows and another reaps.' I sent you to reap that for which you have not labored; others have labored, and you have entered into their labors.'" John 4:35-38 NKJV*

So Jesus is saying I have found My purpose. I am here to reap the harvest. I have already won this woman at the well. I'm here on My purpose. I'm here in My mission, My assignment. Can I say here that we all, as Christians, have one assignment that overshadows all other assignments and work in our life? Jesus said it is right here, He said "*say not that there are four months unto the harvest."* Let's not put this off into the future and procrastinate about it, because the opportunity is right before you, right now, the fields are already white unto harvest.

Our assignment above everything else is to be involved in the harvest, and this is the characteristic of maturity that comes into your and my life when we accept responsibility for the great commission, and those lost souls become our responsibility, not someone else's.

In Bible College, I was required to read a book by Jack Sparks on the new age movement and the cults and occults. In his book, he said that all the cults are the unpaid bills of the church. People who are living in false doctrine and false beliefs, they're the unpaid bills of the church. Those lost people are our responsibility. If you've got unsaved neighbors around where you live, as a Christian, they are your assignment. Your neighbors are whitened harvest fields; start praying and fasting over them, that they may be brought into the kingdom.

Now you might be thinking, I don't like my neighbor; he's a heathen. Every time I go outside, he's got something else negative to say. I don't even like being around him, he's just negative, negative, negative. Right, and he's going to stay that way until you get him saved. Remember your purpose, child of God, the overarching purpose. As Jesus said in John 4, your purpose is to be involved in the harvest of reaching people for Him, because you're reaping wages for eternity. The Bible tells us that God has a special crown as a reward for those who have won souls for the kingdom; who have gone into the harvest field and reaped the harvest of souls.

THE HARVEST FIELD

I interned at a great Pentecostal church running about 700 to 800 in an average worship attendance between my junior and senior year in Bible College. One day, my pastor called me into his office. He reached into his drawer and pulled out 12 visitors' cards and said, *"John, I just want to say thank you and keep up the good work because all 12 of these people that visited here this month put you down as the reason."* What did Jesus say? *"Do you not say, 'There are still four months and then comes the harvest'..."* I'm going to tell you, God intends that we all be involved in the harvest, that's you and me; we're His mouth, we're His hands, we're His feet.

Let me share a story with you from a recent experience

in my own life that will illustrate Jesus' words about the fields being ripe for harvest.

On the way to an international meeting of Apostles, I stopped in Waterboro, South Carolina, to get a bottle of water. I got the water and went to the counter to check out. About that time, the Holy Ghost showed up. I looked at the young woman behind the counter and I asked, "*do you know Jesus, are you saved?*" She said in a kind of not interested way, "*No.*" And I said, "*I'm going to tell you*", and I called her by her name, "*God is here right now.*" By this time, there are three more people in line behind me. So I said again, calling her by name, "*God is here right now, and you know what? This is your day to be saved.*"

We've been praying in our local church prayer meetings that God would release such a grace that it would be easy for people to get saved, easy to get healed, easy to get filled with the Holy Ghost. You should have seen it; this girl could do nothing but get saved. There was nothing standing in the way.

I put my hand out to her and said, "*would you pray with me right now?*" She looked, and then she broke; she put her hand in my hand. She prayed the sinner's prayer after me out loud. She got saved right there behind the cash register.

I was in shock myself because this was not the normal leading somebody to Jesus, this was a sovereign move of God. I was compelled to lead her to Jesus, and she couldn't do anything but get saved. God showed up and everybody was just standing there doing nothing until she got saved. It was a John 4 experience, and it was just powerful!

When we finished and I paid for the water, I said to her, "*God bless you, you're my sister now, and you're saved*". I told her I had a book in the car I wanted to give her and I ran out to get it. If I'd have had my wits about me, I could have cleaned up that whole line right there in the store, because when I turned around they were all looking at me like, what are you going to do? They were feeling it, you could tell they were under conviction, but I was so pumped about her getting saved that I ran out to the car and to get her that book. If I would have just slowed down, they may have all gotten saved. Look for that in your life. Look for it to happen to you like it happened to me. Remember, your overarching purpose is the lost souls that are all around you.

HOW HAVE YOU BEEN DOING WITH EVERY BELIEVER'S GENERAL PURPOSE OF WINNING PEOPLE TO JESUS? SECONDLY, DO YOU KNOW THE INDIVIDUAL PURPOSE GOD HAS GIVEN YOU?

_____

_____

_____

_____

_____

_____

_____

_____

_____

_____

_____

DAY 2

Watch today's video by going to johnpolis.com, clicking on *Discipleship Series* in the main menu and then choosing **LIVING UNSHAKEABLE IN A SHAKING WORLD** Week 3.

WHAT STOOD OUT TO YOU AND WHAT IS GOD SHOWING YOU THROUGH THE VIDEO?

_____

_____

_____

_____

_____

_____

DAY 3

Write **JOHN 4:33-34** in your favorite translation. Go over this passage several times until you can say it from memory and then share it with one person by the end of the day.

JOHN 4:33-34

_____

_____

_____

_____

_____

_____

WHO DID YOU QUOTE YOUR VERSE TO?

_____

DAY 4

IN WHAT WAYS CAN YOU IMPROVE YOUR GENERAL PURPOSE AS A BELIEVER OF WINNING PEOPLE TO JESUS?

_____

_____

_____

_____

_____

_____

_____

_____

_____

DAY 5

IN JUST A FEW SENTENCES, WRITE DOWN WHAT YOU HAVE LEARNED IN THIS CHAPTER AND THEN SHARE IT WITH ONE PERSON BY THE END OF THE DAY.

_____

_____

_____

_____

_____

_____

_____

WHO DID YOU SHARE WITH WHAT YOU LEARNED?

_____

DAY 6

Take time to review everything you have written down that God has shown to you throughout the week. You can also write down any results from your **ACTION STEP**. As leadership expert John Maxwell says, *"Experience is not the best teacher, evaluated experience is"*.

_____

_____

_____

_____

_____

_____

_____

_____

_____

KINGDOM PRINCIPLE #4

FORSAKE SIN

Proverbs 1:10 NKJV
"My son, if sinners entice you, do not consent."

DAY 1

"My son, if sinners entice you, do not consent."
Proverbs 1:10 NKJV

Does Proverbs 1:10 say *"My son if sinners entice you, say, well let me think about it."*? No, it says, *"My son if sinners entice you, say no."* To say no means you've already made a decision about this, there is no contemplation necessary. You don't need to go pray about it and seek the Lord's will. It is sin and it is to be forsaken in our life.

The Bible says in Hebrews that Jesus was anointed above His companions because He loved what was right and hated what was wrong.

> *"You have loved righteousness and hated lawlessness; therefore God, Your God, has anointed You with the oil of gladness more than Your companions."* Hebrews 1:9 NKJV

I guarantee you Jesus knew where He stood when it came to sin. His response was always the same: "NO!" If sinners entice you, say NO, emphatically NO! If the devil tempts you, say NO and say it quick. There's an old saying: *"study long, study wrong!"* You think a little too long and pretty soon the devil talks you into it, convincing you that it will be okay. When it comes to sin, we need to be like Barney Fife and nip it!

FORSAKE SIN, JUST SAY NO

"Blessed is the man who endures temptation; for when he has been approved, he will receive the crown of life which the Lord has promised to those who love Him. Let no one say when he is tempted, "I am tempted by God"; for God cannot be tempted by evil, nor does He Himself tempt anyone. But each one is tempted when he is drawn away by his own desires and enticed. Then, when desire has conceived, it gives birth to sin; and sin, when it is full-grown, brings forth death." James 1:12-15 NKJV

When you have forsaken sin, you've overcome and are strengthened in the process.

BECOME A PILLAR

"He who overcomes, I will make him a pillar in the temple of My God..." Revelation 3:12 NKJV

When you say no to sin and you choose righteousness, and you overcome temptation, God will continually bless and reward your life. But one of the greatest blessings is that you become a pillar in the house of God, in the church, in the body of Christ. You become a support to the whole effort.

WE MUST GET RID OF SIN

Sin weakens, kills, and destroys, that's why the Bible says in 1 Corinthians 5:1-8 "don't even let a little *leaven (sin)* into the house". Now, this passage is not talking about missing the mark [sin]; we all miss the mark from time to time. When that happens, we quickly repent, because that's our immediate response to do what's right in God's sight. For this person, doing right is the habit and sin is the occasional error. But for others, sin is their habit and doing right is the occasional situation. This passage in 1 Corinthians 5 is talking about the habit of sin. As a Pastor, I've had to do some hard things to get the sin out, because just like leaven, sin spreads. I didn't like doing it, but I had to do it, because I have to protect the rest of the flock. How do you deal with sin in someone? You give them a chance to repent and if they don't repent, then they have to go and take the sin with them. That's a mature view of handling the situation; it's not an emotional one, it's a spiritual one, and it has to be done. If there's no repentance, there can be no restoration.

We have probably all seen the effects of when one of our brothers and sisters falls back into sin and goes back out into the world. We feel weakened by that, especially if it was somebody that appeared to be "real spiritual". When this happens, it has a negative effect; it takes out others with it and weakens the whole.

Forsake sin, the Bible says, and God will make you a pillar in His temple. You will be a support and a strength to the body of Christ and that's what God needs us to be, every one of us.

FROM JAMES 4:17, WRITE YOUR OWN DEFINITION OF SIN.

DAY 2

Watch today's video by going to johnpolis.com, clicking on *Discipleship Series* in the main menu and then choosing **LIVING UNSHAKEABLE IN A SHAKING WORLD** Week 4.

WHAT STOOD OUT TO YOU AND WHAT IS GOD SHOWING YOU THROUGH THE VIDEO?

_____

_____

_____

_____

_____

_____

_____

DAY 3

Write **PROVERBS 1:10** in your favorite translation. Go over this passage several times until you can say it from memory and then share it with one person by the end of the day.

PROVERBS 1:10

_____

_____

_____

_____

_____

WHO DID YOU QUOTE YOUR VERSE TO?

_____

DAY 4

ASK GOD, BY HIS HOLY SPIRIT, IF THERE ARE ANY AREAS OF SIN IN YOUR LIFE THAT YOU NEED TO FORSAKE. WHAT STEP DO YOU NEED TO TAKE TO FORSAKE IT?

If you do not know what first step to take, you may need to talk with a trusted Godly leader in your life.

_____

_____

_____

_____

_____

_____

_____

_____

DAY 5

IN JUST A FEW SENTENCES, WRITE DOWN WHAT YOU HAVE LEARNED IN THIS CHAPTER AND THEN SHARE IT WITH ONE PERSON BY THE END OF THE DAY.

_____

_____

_____

_____

_____

_____

_____

WHO DID YOU SHARE WITH WHAT YOU LEARNED?

_____

DAY 6

Take time to review everything you have written down that God has shown to you throughout the week. You can also write down any results from your **ACTION STEP**. As leadership expert John Maxwell says, *"Experience is not the best teacher, evaluated experience is"*.

_____

_____

_____

_____

_____

_____

_____

_____

_____

KINGDOM PRINCIPLE #5

FIT INTO THE BODY OF CHRIST

Ephesians 4:16 NLT
"He makes the whole body fit together perfectly. As each part does its own special work, it helps the other parts grow, so that the whole body is healthy and growing and full of love."

DAY 1

Would you agree with me that it's a whole lot harder to knock over an entire building than it is a single brick? Of course it is. In Ephesians 4:16, the Apostle Paul writes,

> "He makes the whole body fit together perfectly. As each part does its own special work, it helps the other parts grow, so that the whole body is healthy and growing and full of love." Ephesians 4:16 NLT

The King James Version says,

> "From whom the whole body fitly joined together and compacted by that which every joint supplieth, according to the effectual working in the measure of every part, maketh increase of the body unto the edifying of itself in love." Ephesians 4:16 KJV

Here is a kingdom principle: we have to get past our own personal growth and think about the growth of the entire body. See, you can live without the church and the rest of the body of Christ, but it's very much self-centered, and that's the opposite of what Christianity is all about. Christianity is about living for the benefit of other people like Christ did; and so when we find our place, we fit into the body. In doing this, we learn that God has given us something to share to the overall growth of the body, for the edifying, or the building of itself in love.

NO LONGER JUST ABOUT ME.

I don't come to church just for me; I come for everybody else as well. I come because I've got something to share that's going to add to the growth of the body. That's why church membership is so important. When you consider becoming a member of the church, you make a commitment and a covenant to use your talent, your time, and your treasure to help the body grow. Membership says "God has called me here because I have something to supply that the body needs if it is to grow." If I'm supposed to be in a certain church, but I withhold, then it hinders the growth of the body there. Can you see that in the passage found in Ephesians 4?

WE ALL GROW TOGETHER

When you become a part of the body, you become strong and the body becomes stronger. Why? Because you are not standing alone, by yourself, but are surrounded with power, and might, and the gifts and anointing of the other people around you. As previously mentioned, it's a whole lot easier to knock over a single brick than it is an entire building.

Very rarely will you see people that are truly connected to the body of Christ, who are partaking of the grace of others, and sharing the grace God has given them, be shaken off their stand. Find your place in the body of Christ, because you need the body and the body needs you. Being a part of the body helps make you unshakeable. We must find where we fit and begin to share that which God has given us.

WHAT ARE SOME OF THE GIFTS, TALENTS, AND ABILITIES THAT GOD HAS GIVEN YOU THAT YOU BELIEVE WOULD BE A BLESSING TO THE BODY OF CHRIST?

LIVING UNSHAKEABLE IN A SHAKING WORLD

DAY 2

Watch today's video by going to johnpolis.com, clicking on *Discipleship Series* in the main menu and then choosing **LIVING UNSHAKEABLE IN A SHAKING WORLD** Week 5.

WHAT STOOD OUT TO YOU AND WHAT IS GOD SHOWING YOU THROUGH THE VIDEO?

_____

_____

_____

_____

_____

_____

_____

_____

DAY 3

Write **EPHESIANS 4:16** in your favorite translation. Go over this passage several times until you can say it from memory and then share it with one person by the end of the day.

EPHESIANS 4:16

_____

_____

_____

_____

_____

_____

WHO DID YOU QUOTE YOUR VERSE TO?

_____

DAY 4

HOW CAN YOU APPLY THE GIFTS, TALENTS, AND ABILITIES THAT GOD HAS GIVEN YOU IN YOUR LOCAL CHURCH?

_____

_____

_____

_____

_____

_____

_____

_____

_____

DAY 5

IN JUST A FEW SENTENCES, WRITE DOWN WHAT YOU HAVE LEARNED IN THIS CHAPTER AND THEN SHARE IT WITH ONE PERSON BY THE END OF THE DAY.

_____

_____

_____

_____

_____

_____

_____

WHO DID YOU SHARE WITH WHAT YOU LEARNED?

_____

DAY 6

Take time to review everything you have written down that God has shown to you throughout the week. You can also write down any results from your **ACTION STEP**. As leadership expert John Maxwell says, *"Experience is not the best teacher, evaluated experience is"*.

_____

_____

_____

_____

_____

_____

_____

_____

_____

KINGDOM PRINCIPLE #6

FIX YOUR HEART

Psalm 112:7-8 KJV
"He shall not be afraid of evil tidings: his heart is fixed, trusting in the Lord. His heart is established, he shall not be afraid, until he see his desire upon his enemies."

DAY 1

Let's look at the beautiful passage of scripture found in Psalm 112:7,

> *"He will not be afraid of evil tidings; his heart is steadfast, trusting in the Lord." Psalm 112:7 NKJV*

The King James Version says:

> *"He shall not be afraid of evil tidings: his heart is fixed, trusting in the Lord. His heart is established, he shall not be afraid, until he see his desire upon his enemies." Psalm 112:7-8 KJV*

In other words, you're in a battle. There are enemies all around, but your heart is fixed, your heart is established. When the battle is over, your enemies are down and you are still standing. *"and having done all, to stand"* says Ephesians 6:13. How do you stand? You stand by trusting in the Lord. We have to affix ourselves to Him, to be affixed to Him as in super-glued to God. When we put our trust in the Lord, when we affix ourselves to Him, we become unmovable because God is unmovable. He is, in fact, our rock, our fortress; He's the high tower. Affix yourself to Him, and you cannot, will not be moved.

KNOW GOD'S CHARACTER

When you trust in the Lord with all your heart, you do so because you understand the person, nature, and character of God. You cannot trust what you don't know. We may have met Him, but must grow so that we know Him.

We also must be careful not to attempt to trust God at a level that somebody else knows Him. We can't use their relationship with Him as though it was our own, but we can use their relationship as an example for us to follow. We can resolve to one day knowing God like they know Him.

> *"but the people who know their God shall be strong, and carry out great exploits." Daniel 11:32 NKJV*

What does it mean to trust in the Lord? It means we have

come to know Him, His trustworthiness, His dependability, His faithfulness; that He will never fail you; that He will never leave you nor forsake you; that He is on your side. David said in Psalms,

> *"I will say of the Lord, 'He is my refuge and my fortress; My God, in Him I will trust.'... A thousand may fall at your side, and ten thousand at your right hand; but it shall not come near you."* Psalm 91:2&7 NKJV

> *"The Lord is my light and my salvation; whom shall I fear? The Lord is the strength of my life; of whom shall I be afraid? ... Though an army may encamp against me, my heart shall not fear; though war may rise against me, in this I will be confident."* Psalm 27:1&3 NKJV

David knew God, he knew Him and was affixed to Him with confidence, and trust, and consequently, the Bible says in Psalms 112, *"He saw his desire upon his enemies."*

Let's look at Psalm 37:3. This is a beautiful verse which says *"Trust in the Lord and do good."* Once you've cast your cares on the Lord and you've affixed yourself to Him, and you're trusting God to do what He said, then you can busy yourself taking care of things. You can do good now.

> "Trust in the Lord, and do good; dwell in the land, and feed on His faithfulness. Delight yourself also in the Lord, and He shall give you the desires of your heart. Commit your way to the Lord, trust also in Him, and He shall bring it to pass. He shall bring forth your righteousness as the light, and your justice as the noonday. Rest in the Lord, and wait patiently for Him;" Psalm 37:3-7 NKJV

This is what's involved in trust, it's *"I'm at rest now; I've made God responsible for my day, my life, and my outcome. I don't know how or who or when, but I do know what. I know what God is going to do. He's going to do what He said He would do."* When you rest and wait patiently for the Lord, you're trusting in Him, and you don't fret because of Him who prospers in His way. If it looks like the bad guys are getting ahead of you, don't worry about it.

> "Rest in the Lord, and wait patiently for Him; do not fret because of him who prospers in his way, because of the man who brings wicked schemes to pass. Cease from anger, and forsake wrath; do not fret—it only causes harm. For evildoers shall be cut off; but those who wait on the Lord, they shall inherit the earth. For yet a little while and the wicked shall be no more; indeed, you will look carefully for his

place, but it shall be no more. But the meek shall inherit the earth, and shall delight themselves in the abundance of peace. Psalms 37:7-11 NKJV

What an outcome for those people who trust in the Lord, rest in Him and wait patiently for Him.

The last passage I want to share with you is Psalms 16:8,

"I have set the Lord always before me (I'm affixed to Him); because He is at my right hand I shall not be moved." Psalm 16:8 NKJV

We're talking about an unshakeable life, a life that is affixed to God. I assure you if you and will apply these six kingdom principles in this book, your life will become ever more unshakeable and immoveable no matter what the storm, trial, or difficulty that you're going through. This is the promise of God's Word, and it's available for everybody.

DEFINE WHO YOU KNOW GOD TO BE TO YOU.

DAY 2

Watch today's video by going to johnpolis.com, clicking on *Discipleship Series* in the main menu and then choosing **LIVING UNSHAKEABLE IN A SHAKING WORLD** Week 6.

WHAT STOOD OUT TO YOU AND WHAT IS GOD SHOWING YOU THROUGH THE VIDEO?

_____

_____

_____

_____

_____

_____

_____

DAY 3

Write **PSALM 112:7-8** in your favorite translation. Go over this passage several times until you can say it from memory and then share it with one person by the end of the day.

PSALM 112:7-8

_____

_____

_____

_____

_____

_____

WHO DID YOU QUOTE YOUR VERSE TO?

_____

DAY 4

LIST 5 ATTRIBUTES OF GOD THAT ALLOW YOU TO TRUST HIM. ASK HOLY SPIRIT WHAT CHANGES YOU MUST MAKE TO PRODUCE 1 OF THOSE AREAS IN THE NEXT 6 WEEKS.

_____

_____

_____

_____

_____

_____

_____

_____

_____

_____

DAY 5

IN JUST A FEW SENTENCES, WRITE DOWN WHAT YOU HAVE LEARNED IN THIS CHAPTER AND THEN SHARE IT WITH ONE PERSON BY THE END OF THE DAY.

_____

_____

_____

_____

_____

_____

_____

_____

WHO DID YOU SHARE WITH WHAT YOU LEARNED?

_____

DAY 6

Take time to review everything you have written down that God has shown to you throughout the week. You can also write down any results from your **ACTION STEP**. As leadership expert John Maxwell says, *"Experience is not the best teacher, evaluated experience is"*.

_____

_____

_____

_____

_____

_____

_____

_____

ABOUT THE AUTHOR

John Polis was saved and filled with Holy Spirit in 1974 during the Jesus Movement. He attended Dayton Bible College and graduated with a B.A. in Biblical Studies in 1980, after which he became pastor of a Pentecostal church in West Virginia.

In 1983, John had an encounter that transitioned him into the ministry of Apostle. Afterwards, he began to travel as an Evangelist and International Bible Teacher.

Among the works established was Eldoret Bible College in Kenya, Africa, which was birthed in 1998 and has graduated over 2500 students with undergraduate and graduate degrees. Students have planted more than 600 churches throughout Africa to date, some of which have more than 5000 in attendance. John has been a television and radio host for more than 40 years and has authored 18 publications, translated into 6 languages. As President and Founder of Revival Fellowship International, John, and his wife Rebecca, have many spiritual sons and daughters in 13 states and 5 countries. John carries and imparts an Elijah Anointing to prepare the Church for discipling nations as mature sons and daughters. John serves on the Council of Elders for the International Coalition of Apostolic Leaders and is a former United States Marine, being a veteran of the Vietnam War. John and Rebecca have been married 47 years, with 4 children and 9 grandchildren.

MORE BOOKS BY JOHN POLIS

Built Strong:
31 Keys To Spiritual Power.

God Fathers:
How You Can Be One.

Stronger Than Satan:
Understanding Your Authority In Christ.

Victorious:
How To Face, Fight, and Finish Your Battles.

Release The River Within You:
Increasing The Anointing Flow

Put On Your Gloves:
The Five Battles Every Christian Must Win

Apostolic Advice:
Proven Wisdom for Building Strong Foundations in the Local Church

Recycled Believers:
Solving The Mystery of Migrating Sheep

How To Produce Abundance In Your Life:
The Kingdom Secrets Jesus Taught His Disciples

Biblical Headship:
Making Sense of Submission To Authority

The Master Builder:
Wisdom for Today's Apostles

Take My Yoke Upon You:
Fulfilling Your 3 Dimensional Destiny

The Kings Are Coming:
Understanding The Kingly Anointing

BE STRONG IN THE LORD: DISCIPLESHIP SERIES BOOKS BY JOHN POLIS

Living Unshakeable In A Shaking World:
6 Principles For Successful Kingdom Living

Total Victory Is For You:
5 Smooth Stones To Slay Your Giants

The Love Of God

How To Obtain Strong Faith

Spiritual Warfare:
No Place For Satan

For these and additional resources to help you in your spiritual growth, go to ***www.johnpolis.com***.

JOHNPOLIS
INTERNATIONAL

Helping create and shape great futures
JOHNPOLIS.COM

THE COMPLETE SCHOOL OF THE HOLY SPIRIT

Benefit from 40 years of Spirit filled life and ministry with this 14 hour course produced by Dr John Polis.

This in-depth study of the Person and Work of Holy Spirit, punctuated with prophetic impartation, life encounters and sound teaching, will be an essential equipping tool for individuals and churches.

AVAILABLE ON USB, DVD, Or CD **$99** +shipping

THE COMPLETE SCHOOL OF FAITH

TOPICS INCLUDE: What Faith Is, How Faith Comes, Believing with the Heart, Doubt in the Heart, Fully Persuaded Faith, The Gift of Faith, The Sixth Sense, Destroying Things That Are Not, Faith & Patience, What You Say Will Save You, and more.

Enjoy 13 sessions of a special anointing God poured out upon Dr. John as he ministered prophetically on the subject of faith. Receive revelation and an impartation of the spirit of faith. Over 10 hours of teaching with syllabus included.

AVAILABLE ON USB, DVD, Or CD **$99** +shipping

THE COMPLETE SCHOOL OF HEALING

The Complete School of Healing is the result of more than 35 years of study on the subject of Divine Healing. YOU WILL LEARN ABOUT: A Scriptural Basis for Healing, The Origin and Nature of Sickness, God's Will and Healing, Methods of Receiving Divine Healing, and When God Doesn't Seem to Answer.

AVAILABLE ON USB, DVD, Or CD **$99** +shipping

VICTORIOUS

Isaiah 54:17 says, "No weapon that is formed against thee shall prosper; and every tongue that shall rise against thee in judgment thou shalt condemn." In this 5 part series you will learn the secrets of successful spiritual warfare and defeating the giants in your life.

AVAILABLE ON USB Or CD **$30** +shipping

WANT TO HEAR MORE OF DR. JOHN?

Download the free Faith Church International App by searching your app store for "Faith Church Int" or by scanning the QR Code.

REVIVAL FELLOWSHIP INTERNATIONAL

Revival Fellowship International (RFI) is called to preach and teach RESTORATION THEOLOGY to the Body of Christ, presenting "every man complete in Christ." This is being done through meetings, conferences, publications, media and bible colleges here and abroad.

A second apostolic responsibility of RFI is in the raising up of a new generation of spiritual leaders as "spiritual sons and daughters" who will lead restoration revival as it continues to the coming of Christ. We offer a credentialing process that brings people into covenant relationships that are necessary for impartation to take place.

The Elijah Anointing has been imparted to RFI and is the generational inheritance given to those in covenant connection with the movement. Those apostolic leaders with an Elijah anointing are the true spiritual fathers of today's church. By running with this vision, RFI is fulfilling the prophecy of restoration in Acts 3:19-21..."Heaven must retain Him until the restoration of all things". **For more information go to www.rfiusa.org**

Made in the USA
Middletown, DE
01 February 2022